Africa

A Buddy Book
by

Cheryl Striveildi

ABDO
Publishing Company

VISIT US AT
www.abdopub.com

Published by Buddy Books, an imprint of ABDO Publishing Company, 4940 Viking Drive, Edina, Minnesota 55435. Copyright © 2003 by Abdo Consulting Group, Inc. International copyrights reserved in all countries. No part of this book may be reproduced in any form without written permission from the publisher.

Printed in the United States.

Edited by: Christy DeVillier
Contributing Editors: Matt Ray, Michael P. Goecke
Graphic Design: M. Hosley
Image Research: Deborah Coldiron
Photographs: Corbis, Corel, Digital Stock, Eyewire, Photodisc, Photospin, PowerPhotos

Library of Congress Cataloging-in-Publication Data

Striveildi, Cheryl, 1971-
    Continents. Africa / Cheryl Striveildi.
        p. cm.
    Includes index.
    Summary: A very brief introduction to the geography, various regions, and wildlife of Africa.
    ISBN 1-57765-958-9
        1. Africa—Juvenile literature. [1. Africa.] I. Title: Africa. II. Title.

DT3 .S84 2003
916—dc21

2002074659

Table of Contents

Seven Continents

Water covers most of the earth. Land covers the rest. The earth has seven main land areas, or continents. The seven continents are:

 North America

 Africa

 South America

 Asia

 Europe

 Australia

 Antarctica

There is much to see in Africa.

Africa is the second-largest continent. It covers about 11,609,000 square miles (30,065,000 sq km).

Africa's people have a rich mix of customs and languages. This continent is also famous for its wild animals.

Where Is Africa?

The equator is an imaginary line. It divides the earth into two equal halves. The Northern Hemisphere is the top half of the earth. The Southern Hemisphere is the bottom half. Africa lies in both hemispheres.

The Atlantic Ocean is west of Africa. The Indian Ocean is east of Africa.

Africa lies south of Europe. Between these two continents is the Mediterranean Sea.

Africa lies southwest of Asia. The Red Sea lies between these two continents.

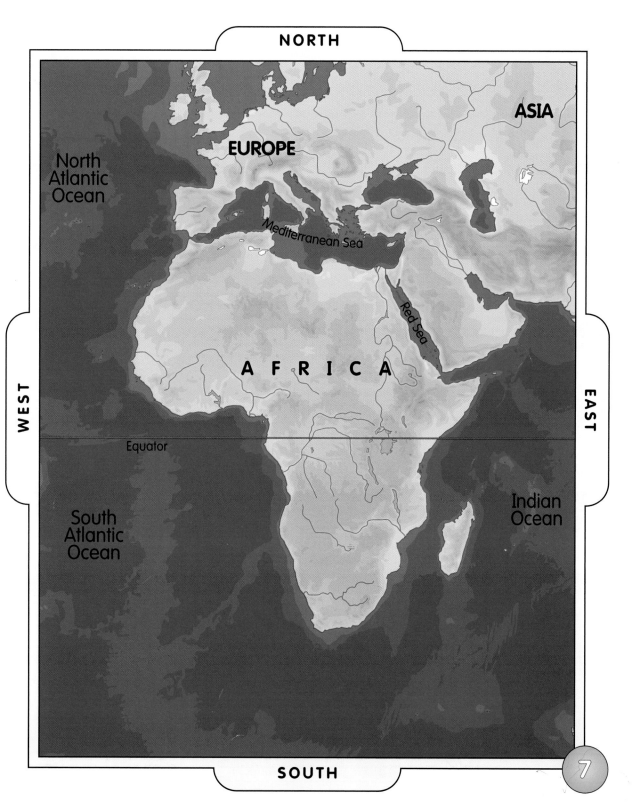

ASIA

EUROPE

North
Atlantic
Ocean

Mediterranean Sea

Red Sea

A F R I C A

Equator

Indian
Ocean

South
Atlantic
Ocean

Countries

There are 53 countries in Africa. Sudan is the largest African country. It is in eastern Africa. The longest river in the world flows through Sudan. It is the Nile River.

The African country with the most people is Nigeria. More than 100 million people live there. It is on the west coast of Africa. Millions of Africans live in Egypt and Ethiopia, too.

The Nile River also flows through Egypt.

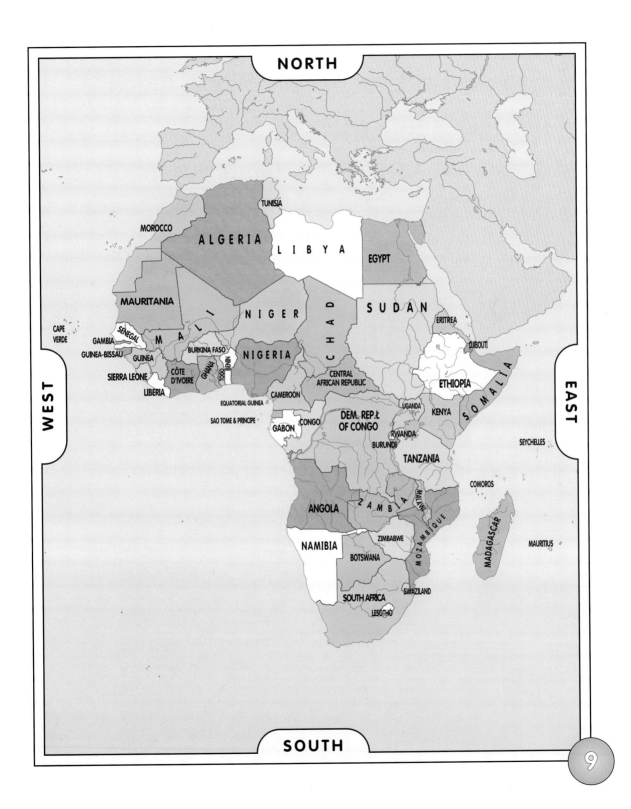

Many kinds of people live in Africa. There are more than 800 ethnic groups. The people of each ethnic group share a common way of life. Clothes, language, and other customs may change from group to group.

More than 1,000 different languages are spoken in Africa. A few of them are Arabic, Swahili, and French. Some African languages have clicking sounds.

Most people in Africa live away from cities.

Africa has many ethnic groups.

Largest Desert

There are three big deserts in Africa. They are the Sahara, the Kalahari, and the Namib. The Kalahari and the Namib are in southwest Africa. The Sahara Desert is in northern Africa.

Deserts get less than 10 inches (25 cm) of rain each year. The Sahara is the largest desert in the world. It is almost as big as the United States. The dry Sahara Desert is hot during the day. It is cold at night.

It is not easy living in the Sahara Desert. There are not many roads or cities. But some people do live there. Many of these people are nomads. Nomads travel from place to place. Many Saharan nomads keep sheep or camels. Some gather and sell desert salt.

Many people of the Sahara travel on camels.

Camels can store water for many days.

Many animals live in Africa's deserts. There are fennec foxes, caracals, and horned vipers. Fennec foxes have big ears. They stay under ground during the day. Caracals are wild, meat-eating cats. The horned viper is a snake with special horns on its head.

Caracal

Desert Oasis

Where do people and animals in the desert get water? They go to a desert oasis. An oasis has water from under the ground. The land around an oasis is green. The Sahara Desert has many oases.

Date palms and other plants grow near oases.

Rain Forests

Most of Africa's rain forests are in central Africa. These are the Congo Basin rain forests. This is the second-biggest rain forest area in the world.

Rain forests get more than 80 inches (203 cm) of rain each year. They are tropical places. The Congo Basin rain forests have swamps and evergreen forests. The forests are full of mahogany trees. Thousands of different plants grow there, too.

Many kinds of animals live in Africa's rain forests. There are monkeys, gorillas, lemurs, okapi, baboons, and elephants. The biggest frog in the world lives there, too. It is the Goliath frog.

Lowland gorilla

Baboon

Okapi

Lemur

Elephants live in Africa's rain forests.

African Oil Palms

African oil palms grow in western Africa. These trees have oil palm fruit. The fruit's oils are used in soap, shampoo, and foods. The tree's sap can be made into wine.

Savannas

Africa has large areas of grasslands called savannas. These savannas are south of the Sahara Desert. There is savanna land in southern Africa, too.

African savanna

Lions live on the African savanna.

The African savanna has grasses, bushes, and few trees. Summers there are warm and dry. The winters are not very cold.

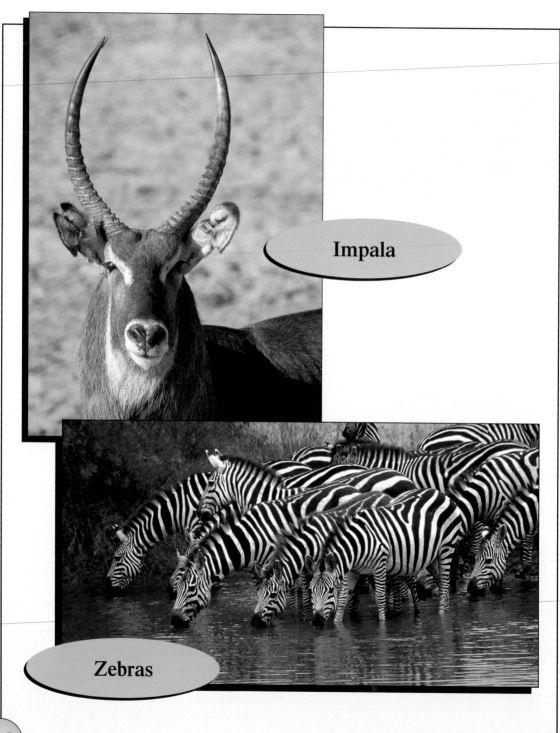

Impala

Zebras

Elephants, zebras, antelopes, lions, and cheetahs live on the African savannas. Cheetahs are wild cats. They can run as fast as 70 miles (113 km) per hour.

Elephant

Cheetah

Visiting Africa

"Going on safari" means taking a special trip. Many people go on safari to the Serengeti National Park. It is on the Serengeti Plain of northern Tanzania. The Serengeti National Park is 5,700 square miles (14,763 sq km).

Masai warriors of Tanzania

The Serengeti National Park is famous for its wild animals. Wildebeests, zebras, cheetahs, lions, giraffes, elephants, hippos, rhinos, baboons, and gazelles live there.

Rhinos (left) and baboons (right) live at the Serengeti National Park.

Mount Kilimanjaro

Another beautiful place in Africa is Mount Kilimanjaro. It stands in northern Tanzania.

Mount Kilimanjaro is the highest mountain in Africa. Many people enjoy climbing it.

Many people like to visit the pyramids of Egypt, too. Long ago, Egyptians built these stone pyramids for their rulers. Some Egyptian pyramids are more than 4,000 years old. The biggest one is about 450 feet (137 m) tall.

Africa's Egyptian pyramids are an amazing sight.

Africa

- Africa is the second-largest continent.

- Africa's Sahara Desert is the biggest desert in the world.

- The longest river in the world is Africa's Nile River.

- Mount Kilimanjaro is the highest mountain in Africa.

- Lake Assal is the lowest point in Africa.

- Africa's biggest country is Sudan.

- About 800 million people live in Africa.

Important Words

continent one of the earth's seven main land areas.

customs the way of life common to a group of people. Language, food, clothes, and religion are some customs.

equator the imaginary line that divides the earth into two equal halves.

ethnic group a group of people that share customs and a common background.

hemisphere one half of the earth.

nomads people that travel from place to place.

savannas grasslands.

tropical weather that is warm and wet.

Web Sites

Would you like to learn more about Africa?
Please visit ABDO Publishing Company on the World Wide Web to find web site links about Africa. These links are routinely monitored and updated to provide the most current information available.

www.abdopub.com

Index